This Book was Donated Through the
Reading is an Investment Program

This program is brought to you by:

Vermont State Treasurer's Office
TD Bank Charitable Foundation
Windham Foundation
Vermont Student Assistance Corporation

Reading is an Investment
A Program of the Vermont State Treasurer's Office

The Soda Bottle School

A True Story of Recycling, Teamwork,
and One Crazy Idea

Seño Laura Kutner
and Suzanne Slade

Illustrated by
Aileen Darragh

Each morning, the Guatemalan sun climbed the mighty Tuncaj Volcano to wake the small, sleepy town of Granados below. Fernando thought nothing exciting ever happened in his village. But then something amazing happened. And it all started with one crazy idea.

That day began like every other—Mamá got ready for work while Abuela fixed black beans and eggs and Abuelo told his stories.

Then Fernando walked the steep hill to school.
Up, up, up he climbed until he spied the
school's metal roof.

Fernando joined some friends playing fútbol before school. As he ran across the playground, he waved to his favorite teacher, Seño Laura.

Before she'd moved to the village, Fernando was the only person in the whole school who wore glasses. But not any more. Seño Laura wore them, too. Their glasses helped them see lots of things: delicate spider webs, brilliant hummingbirds, colorful rainbows in the distance.

And sometimes, they even saw possibilities—new ideas—others didn't.

The morning bell rang out.

Two hundred students squished
inside the small schoolhouse.

Two grades squashed into one classroom.

Two children squeezed behind one desk.

The walls between the classrooms didn't reach the ceiling,
so hundreds of voices echoed through the school. All day.
Every day. Some days it was too noisy to think.

After morning lessons, matemáticas and ciencia, it was time for recreo. Fernando ran into the wide, grassy schoolyard. He found Seño Laura sitting on a large frame made of red metal. The frame was the empty shell of classrooms that had not been finished. Years before, the village had started building new rooms, but there wasn't enough money to finish them. But there was one thing Granados had plenty of—trash.

The problem began when products in fancy packages started arriving from other countries. Now old water bottles, soda bottles, chip bags, and grocery sacks littered the land. The town didn't have recycling centers. No garbage trucks. Not even a dump. There was no place to put their trash.

Seño Laura took a sip of cold soda,
then set her bottle beside a metal bar.
The plastic bottle sparkled in the
sunlight. It was exactly the same
width as the metal bar.

And that's when it happened—
the crazy idea.

Seño Laura ran to the principal's office and told her all about it.

"I love this idea," Principal Reyna said. "Let's get started right away!"

Then Seño Laura and the principal visited Fernando's classroom.

"Our trash piles are too big. Our school is too small," Seño Laura said. "Do you think we could build a new school with old bottles and trash?"

"That would take a lot of bottles," one student said.

"It sounds like a lot of work," worried another.

"I'm not sure we could do it," sighed a third.

Fernando pushed his glasses up on his nose and peered outside. He studied the trash surrounding the school. He imagined a row of colorful bottles on the metal frame. He pictured hundreds and hundreds of bottles stacked on each other. Then he saw it— a new, bigger school.

A school with enough room for everyone!

Fernando couldn't wait to start. His excitement spread to his friends, family, and neighbors. Before long, the whole town was talking about the school's crazy idea. Everyone wanted to help. Students. Teachers. Papás. Mamás. Abuelos. Abuelas. Even the mayor!

Children started collecting bottles. Near school. In town. Beside fields. Fernando lugged bags of sticky bottles to school. He washed each one and set the bottles in the sun to dry. Day after day, the bottle pile grew. Students filled Principal Reyna's office with bottles, leaving only a narrow path to her desk.

The empty bottles weren't strong enough to build a wall, so students stuffed the bottles with trash to create eco-ladrillos. Using small sticks, they shoved old chip bags, grocery sacks, and plastic trash into the bottles.

The more eco-ladrillos the children made, the cleaner and more beautiful their village became.

Stick

Bottle

Trash

eco-ladrillo

Before long, they'd cleaned up the entire town!

Then bad news blew through the village like an August caliente wind.

The bottles had been counted. They needed thousands more.

The school could not be finished. Again.

But Fernando still believed in the crazy idea. His friends did, too.

So they strapped on their sandals and walked miles to nearby towns.

They gathered more bottles and trash. And they kept stuffing.

Fernando stuffed bottles before school. During recess. After school. He stuffed until his hands blistered. After six long months, the town finally had enough eco-ladrillos—6,000 in all! It was time to start building.

The mayor bought bales of chicken wire. Students rolled wire over the metal bars and tied it securely in place. They left two huge holes for windows. The Guatemalan sun would give them plenty of free light.

Fernando stacked bottles between the wire, straight and tall. When the wall grew over his head, he climbed a homemade ladder and kept stacking. Soon the wall was as high as a mighty Ceiba tree. Children stuffed trash between the bottles to make the wall solid and secure.

Villagers gathered to admire their rainbow-colored walls. But the school wasn't finished yet.

The children dragged heavy bags of powdery cement inside.
They sifted rocky sand through screens. They mixed water into the
fine sand and cement powder until it turned into a sticky paste.

Fernando threw a glob of cement on a wall. Splat!
Students covered the plastic walls. Splat! Splat! Splat!
Local masons poured thick cement floors. Village welders
installed windows and doors.

Then the children grabbed brushes and painted the walls with bright, rainbow colors. Some rooms were blue like the wide, endless sky. They painted the outside with Principal Reyna's favorite color—orange.

After fifteen months, the school was finally finished. Ugly trash had turned into a beautiful school. And Granados was cleaned up! Joy filled the village. A joy so big it had to be celebrated. The town decided to throw a huge fiesta.

Fernando and his friends decorated the school with streamers and signs. The principal gave a speech. The mayor cut a thick, red ribbon. Then hundreds of feet danced to the powerful beat of Mayan songs.

Papás cheered. Mamás cried. But Fernando just smiled.

His school was exactly as he and Seño Laura had pictured it—big and beautiful—with plenty of room for everyone.

But that isn't the end of this story.

Nearby villages heard about the school made of trash. They began picking up their old bottles and bags, too. They used them to build new schools, recycling centers, fences, and more.

And it all began with one crazy idea!

A Note
from the Authors,
Seño Laura Kutner
and
Suzanne Slade

The tiny town of Granados (population 847) had two huge problems in 2007. Their trash piles were too big and their school was too small. So the villagers gathered. They asked questions. They searched for solutions. There were no easy answers, but they didn't give up hope. They knew they'd solve these problems like those in past generations—together. And that's exactly what they did.

One day during recess, Seño Laura noticed her plastic soda bottle was the same width as the unfinished red metal frame. She recalled a local group called Pura Vida Atitlan had stuffed plastic bottles with trash to create eco-bricks, or eco-ladrillos. No one knew if that technique would work with the school's existing metal frame, but the villagers decided to try.

The main thing that turned this "crazy idea" into a new school was teamwork. More than two hundred children at the Escuela Oficial Urbana Mixta de Granados, ages five to fifteen, helped build the school, along with teachers, parents, grandparents, and other villagers. Working seven days a week, students collected bottles and plastic trash, cleaned and stuffed bottles, installed chicken wire, stacked bottles, filled holes, sifted sand, mixed cement, plastered walls, and painted. The mayor paid for chicken wire and cement. Local engineers dug the foundation, welded metal, and put on the final layers of cement. An organization called Hug It Forward heard about the project and provided funds to finish the walls, floors, windows, and doors.

This story shares the hard work and determination of an enthusiastic fourth-grade student, Fernando José, and his classmates. Throughout the entire fifteen-month project, Fernando had a helpful attitude and a huge smile on his face. The work was exhausting but none of the students quit, because like Fernando, they loved their school and they wanted to make sure it had enough room for everyone. When the school was finally finished on October 29, 2009, the town threw a huge celebration.

After the project was completed, the villagers started thinking about trash differently. They looked for ways to reduce their use of plastics, and tried new ideas to recycle waste. Businesses stopped burning their huge piles of trash, which gave off a black, toxic smoke, and found alternative ways to dispose of their waste. The Granados school inspired nearby villages too. So far, more than twenty-five additional villages have built their own bottle schools.

Top Left: Seño Laura and friends stand in front of a wall of eco-ladrillos.

Right: Seño Laura, Fernando, and other students of the Soda Bottle School.

TILBURY HOUSE, PUBLISHERS

12 Starr Street
Thomaston, Maine 04861
800-582-1899
www.tilburyhouse.com

First hardcover edition: May 2014 • 10 9 8 7 6 5 4
ISBN 978-0-88448-371-7

DEDICATIONS

This book is dedicated to Fernando José García, Reyna Floridalma Alvarado de
Ramírez, and Zonia and Milder García. Their friendship, generosity, and
compassion are what made this project a success, and they continue to inspire
me every day. —LK

To the inspiring Granados community, and in fond memory of Laura Crawford,
beloved teacher and friend —SS

To my daughters, Catherine, Julia, and Elizabeth —AD

A portion of Laura Kutner's profits will go to support environmental education through
Trash for Peace, a nonprofit organization she founded upon her return to the United States.
Resources and activities for teachers can be found on the Trash for Peace website,
www.trashforpeace.org

A portion of Suzanne Slade's profits will go to Hug It Forward (www.hugitforward.org)
to support the construction of more bottle schools in Guatemala.

Library of Congress Cataloging-in-Publication Data
Slade, Suzanne.
The soda bottle school : a true story about recycling, teamwork, and one crazy idea / Suzanne Slade and
Laura Kutner ; illustrations by Aileen Darragh. -- First hardcover edition.
pages cm
Audience: K to Grade 3
ISBN 978-0-88448-371-7 (hardcover : alk. paper)
1. Recycling industry--Juvenile literature. 2. Teams in the workplace--Juvenile literature.
3. Thought and thinking. I. Kutner, Laura, 1984- II. Darragh, Aileen, 1962- illustrator. III. Title.
HD9975.A2S63 2014
363.72'82--dc23
                        2013040075
Designed by Ann Casady
Printed in China by Shenzhen Caimei Printing Company through Four Colour Print Group, Louisville,
Kentucky (May 2016) 66887-0 / SCP 040616.6

Here's how to say
some of the Spanish words in
the story, and what they mean:

Abuela (a-buey-la):
grandmother

Abuelo (a-buey-lo):
grandfather

Seño (sen-yo):
a term of respect

Matemáticas
(ma-tee-mat-ee-cas):
mathematics

Ciencia (see-yen-see-ya):
science

Recreo (re-cray-o): recess

Ladrillo (la-dree-yo): brick